*Prayers Before
and After
Bereavement*

Prayers Before and After Bereavement

Michael Hollings
and Etta Gullick

McCRIMMON
Great Wakering Essex

First published in Great Britain in 1985 by
Mayhew McCrimmon Ltd
10-12 High Street
Great Wakering Essex

© 1985 Mayhew McCrimmon Ltd

ISBN 0 85597 381 1

Cover design Paul Shuttleworth
Typesetting by Barry Sarling, Rayleigh
Printed by Mayhew McCrimmon Printers Ltd
Great Wakering

Contents

I Approaching the death of one I love	7
Why this waiting?	8
Christ died as we must die	8
When death is near	9
For the dying	13
II The immediate shock of death	14
III Between death and the funeral	19
For strength in parting	20
Into your hands…	21
At the death of a young person	22
Hope in God	22
The day of the funeral	24
IV Anger and guilt	26
V Is there a life after death?	30
VI Realising loss and learning to live in hope	33

VII Resurrection	41
Appendix: Short prayers	47
Epilogue	49
Acknowledgements	51

I

Approaching the death of one I love

For each of us at different times of life there come one or two or several numbing kicks in the stomach, when we are told that someone we love has an incurable cancer; has a terminal disease; has probably only weeks or months to live.

Some people panic; some present a stiff upper lip and carry on; some feel the person threatened with death should not know; some want to share but are persuaded by doctors or welfare workers against the patient being told.

Our conviction as a result of suffering bereavement and sharing bereavement with individuals and families is that, whenever possible, all concerned should know. It avoids hypocrisy, 'happy chat' which covers up the situation.

More positively, as human beings God has made us capable of facing pain, disaster and even death. It undermines the true dignity of a person to deny her/him the right to know. Also, from frequent experience, days, weeks, months and even years have sprung from the moment of truth, and been shared and immensely enjoyed. Relationships which seemed as deep as possible have deepened. We offer these prayers for *you*, individually or together. Some at least we hope you can share. If you can, you will realise why we want you to enter into sharing. God be with you.

Why this waiting?

Lord, help me to understand why you let people linger between life and death so long. This waiting is hard for us and for them, yet it may be important to you. Are you working on them, purifying them and us? A friend suggested that it was at such times that you unravelled the knots and tightnesses which grow in us, and that such waiting was right and good. Could you please help me to see a little of what you are doing when situations seem simply futile and useless to us?

Christ died as we must die

Lord, I keep reminding myself you were a real man, really dying in great agony, and that your mother and some of your dearest friends actually stood and watched you die.

I am here now at the foot of my personal cross watching the one I love die. I am torn in two, for I long for him/her to live; I dread life without him/her; but for his/her sake I wish it were over, the suffering ended, and him/her released.

O Lord, who loved your mother and your friends so dearly, help and support us in our agony.

When death is near

Blessed are you Lord, my God, spirit of the universe, who brought me across the bridge of life. When the dim light of my own self will sink and merge within the light which illumines the world and eternity, I shall conclude the order of my days.

In this twilight glow of my life, I stand before the dawn of my new sun with tense consciousness, a man about to die and to live, who feels at one with the universe and eternity, as in the ancient words: 'Hear, Israel, the Lord our God, the Lord is One.' Blessed is the God of life and death, of light and love.

Nachman Syrkin

When Adam saw for the first time the sun go down and an ever deepening gloom enfold creation, his mind was filled with terror. God then took pity on him, and endowed him with the divine intuition to take two stones — the name of one was 'Darkness' and the name of the other 'Shadow of Death' — and rub them against each other, and so discover fire. Thereupon Adam exclaimed with grateful joy: 'Blessed be the creator of light!'

Talmud

Prayers to be said together

Lord, it was a terrible shock when the doctor told us we must face the fact that N's illness is terminal. They will go on trying, and we will fight it together.

Give us courage and strength and some deep peace inside us. Help us to share everything even more fully than before, to be entirely open. Let us enjoy the lovely times passed, and give us the wonder of each other in the present moment. Give us your Spirit of wisdom and love.

We are so truly thankful for all you have given us. Even in this moment we want to say 'Thank you'. Lead us through this time, however long or short it may be, in trust. And, Lord, increase our belief and hope that ahead of us both there will be an eternity of love together and with you.

The one thing each of us can be quite certain of reaching in life is death, Lord. There is no other complete certainty. Is this why I want so often to put death out of my mind? Death is too unknown and yet too real a presence — a future state of dark anxiety and dread. Yet I believe that you, Lord, are the Lord of Life...you have promised eternal life.

Why then am I restless, and why do I fear? Is it that I do not know you well enough to trust you, to want to be with you for ever? Lord, draw me closer to you and so to those I love who are with you. Teach me to trust myself to you.

Into your hands, Father, I commit myself and all those I love.

The Lord's my Shepherd, I'll not want,
he makes me down to lie
in pastures green. He leadeth me
the quiet waters by.
My soul he doth restore again,
and me to walk doth make
within the paths of righteousness,
e'en for his own name's sake.
Yea, though I walk in death's dark vale,
yet will I fear none ill.
For thou art with me, and thy rod
and staff me comfort still.

My table thou hast furnishéd
in presence of my foes,
my head thou dost with oil anoint,
and my cup overflows.
Goodness and mercy all my life
Shall surely follow me.
And in God's house for evermore
my dwelling-place shall be.

Psalm 23 (from the Scottish Psalter 1650)

Soul of Christ sanctify me,
Body of Christ save me,
Blood of Christ inebriate me,
Water from the side of Christ wash me,
Splendour of the face of Christ illuminate me,
Passion of Christ strengthen me,
Sweat from the face of Christ heal me,
O good Jesus, hear me,
Within thy wounds hide me,
Suffer me not to be separated from thee,
From the malicious enemy defend me,
In the hour of my death call me,
And bid me come to thee,
That with thy saints and angels I may praise thee,
For ever and ever.

Pope John XXII (1249-1334)

Lord, make me an instrument of thy peace.
Where there is hatred, let me sow love;
Where there is injury, pardon;
Where there is doubt, faith;
Where there is despair, hope;
Where there is darkness, light; and
Where there is sadness, joy.
O Divine Master, grant that I may not so much
  seek to be consoled, as to console;
To be understood as to understand;
To be loved as to love;
For it is in giving that we receive;
It is in pardoning that we are pardoned.
And it is in dying that we are born to eternal life.

St Francis of Assisi (c 1181-1226)

For the dying

O Lord Jesus, who in thy last agony didst commend thy spirit into the hands of thy heavenly Father: have mercy on... who is dying; may death be unto him/her the gate of everlasting life; give him/her the assurance of thy presence even in the dark valley; for thy name's sake who art the resurrection and the life, to whom be glory for ever and ever.

Adapted from the Sarum Primer

II

The immediate shock of death

Jesus tells us to watch and pray, because we do not know at what hour the Master will come. We all know, without doubt, the horror of the unexpected. Perhaps not everyone realises that when death has been foreseen, and sharing has been very deep, death is still an earthquake. No planning or sharing can totally cut out the shock.

Because we are individuals we do not react according to a pattern. It is essential at the shock of death that you should be yourself. If you have shared, if the suffering has been long, if you could see no future rehabilitation even if death was averted, you may thank God the ordeal of dying is over.

But you may have been taken totally by surprise, you may have been praying hope against hope for a cure, you may be completely disillusioned with God, angry at his failure to respond to your prayer. You may also have some immediate feeling of guilt, or want to run away and forget. There are many different reactions.

Thoughts and prayers

There is no magical anaesthetic for the pain of grief. We cannot give to the bereaved the one thing they most want; we cannot call back Lazarus, or Bert or Harry from the dead. The bereaved know that. They know 'There is nothing you can say'. And they have seen others turn away, embarrassed by their uselessness. But anyone who turns towards the widow and the widower and gives confidence that they do have something to offer at moments of utter despair helps to reassure them that all is not lost. Goodness is not gone from the world because one who meant so much is no longer present. The loss of one trusted person need not undermine trust in all of those who remain.

Colin Murray Parkes

The day of death is when two worlds meet with a kiss; this world going out, the future world coming in.

Jose ben Abin

Whom have I in heaven but you?
Beside you, I desire nothing on earth.
My flesh and heart may fail
but God is the rock of my heart
and my portion forever.

For those who go far from you perish,
You destroy all who betray your trust.
But for me, the nearness of God is my good.
I have made the Lord God my refuge
that I might tell of all your works.

Psalm 73

Lord Jesus Christ, grief can be very messy. My eyes are red and my face is swollen and my body heaves with sobbing. All I want to do is to hide away in a dark corner so that no one can see me.

The prophet said of you that you were a man of sorrows and acquainted with grief, and as one from whom men hide their faces, so you must understand how it is with me. No one can possibly want to be with such a pitiful object as I am now. I feel unclean and not quite human. I would like a hand to hold, someone to embrace, but there is none; but you at least understand. Let me be aware of the warmth and comfort of your nearness. Amen.

A great loneliness has come over my mind and heart, Lord. Much as I love, much as I know I am loved, I am an individual, and now I am so very much alone. I have lost the closeness of that human presence. Lord, please give me now and always an assurance of your presence, the comfort of your love. I know I must not be greedy or expect the wrong expression of your love. In your plan you take away those we love and you seem to absent yourself. I believe you do it to help me grow. I try to trust you and understand...but O Lord, it is so hard to be alone!

O God, I give thee back my loved one and give thee thanks for the years thou didst entrust him/her to my care.

Charles F. Whitson

Save me, O God, for the waters are come in even
    unto my soul.
I stick fast in the deep mire, where no ground is,
I am come into deep waters, so that the floods run
    over me.
I am weary of crying: my throat is dry;
My sight faileth for waiting so long upon my God...

Take me out of the mire, that I sink not;
O let me be delivered from them that hate me,
   and out of the deep waters.
Let not the water flood drown me, neither let the
   deep swallow me up;
and let not the pit shut her mouth upon me.
Hear me, O Lord, for thy loving-kindness is
   comfortable;
Turn thee unto me according to the multitude of
   thy mercies.

Psalm 69 1-3 and 15-17

Lord, I've just seen his/her body. At first I was shocked and didn't want to look at it, and then I wasn't afraid any longer. It's like looking at an empty house once lived in by somebody I loved. It's dreadfully sad and somehow there is tremendous hope. The living spirit which made this rigid body something marvellous must be with you — what else could happen?

   Somehow death seems a little less frightening. Keep helping me to hope and trust so I shall not be so frightened of death.

The face of God

Out of the hidden depths of my soul
To you, O hidden God, I cry — hear my prayer...

Only show me your face, let me see your face!
...I would drink of the source of all sources,
I long to bathe in the light of all lights...
Your face, *your* face I crave to see.

Jewish prayer

III

Between death and the funeral

The days between death and the funeral can be a mixture of deep grief, numbness, a struggling realisation of loss — and a desire to be busy with making arrangements, so that everything will be as fitting and perfect as possible for the funeral rites, and for family sharing. Relatives and friends have to be notified, and some accommodated, registrars and undertakers interviewed and the funeral service planned.

During these days we need to pray and plan, to be together with others and alone. There is a mixture of desire for human closeness and support, with a pull sometimes towards solitude and aloneness. We vary between personal, individual sorrow and the wish to be able to make the last positive acts of love and care which we can do in this world for the one we have loved and lost.

For strength in parting

Lord Jesus, in your life on earth you knew all about partings. You had to leave your home and family to go into the wider world, to preach the good news. You had to part company with the establishment of your time; Lazarus died and you wept; your closest friends deserted you in your hour of need — one even betrayed you to your enemies. But though you knew partings, they did not overwhelm you. In love you went through their painfulness. Strengthen me in the pain of the parting I have just undergone. Let me feel your support and know that in some strange way my prayer will be deepened through my pain. Then, through my experience of your closeness and love, help me to help others when they are struck by the grief of death and parting.

I am so miserable and the pain is so great that I do not know what to do. Friends tell me to keep busy. Yet even when I am busy I have a deep nagging ache that will not go away. Someone has told me there is no cure for the pain of the death of someone one loves. Nothing I take or do will reduce the agony. Yet, Lord, the love you have shown me and still show me, does give me hope. It is not easy to say how this is so but I thank you for this dim sense of faint understanding.

Into your hands

Lord God, you have created N and me and all men, women and children. You have made us for yourself. I believe that many of those I love are in your care, because they have died in this world and gone to your kingdom. I so much hope and trust that they are now in the peace and joy of your love. But at this time I ask you especially for N, whom you have just taken from me. I loved him/her so much. I miss him/her so much. Lord, I trust him/her to your mercy, your forgiveness and your love.

God full of compassion whose presence is over us, grant perfect rest beneath the shelter of your presence with the holy and pure on high who shine as the lights of heaven to .... who has gone to her/his everlasting home. Master of mercy, cover her/him in the shelter of your wings forever, and bind her/his soul into the gathering of life. It is the Lord who is her/his heritage. May she/he be at peace in her/his place of rest. Amen.

Forms of Prayer for Jewish Worship

At the death of a young person

Now and then in my life, Lord Jesus, I meet a sad, sudden and early death. You raised the son of the widow to life. But this doesn't seem to happen in my experience. I want to pray now, Lord, for N. She/he died before her/his time, young in years. Help me, help the family and her/his friends to accept this numbing loss, to comfort each other, not to lose faith in you, but to trust and love you still.

Hope in God

As a deer longs for running streams,
so my soul longs for You, my God.

My soul thirsts for God, the living God.

'When shall I come and appear before God?'

My tears have been my food, by day and night,
as all day long men say to me, 'Where is your God?'

These things I remember, as I pour out my soul —
how I would pass by with the throng
leading them to the house of God,
with voices raised in joy and praise, the noise of celebration.

Why are you cast down my soul, and why do you moan within me?
Hope in God! I praise Him still, for the salvation of His presence.

My God, when my soul is cast down within me, I think of You.
From the land of Jordan, and the Hermons, from the hill of Mitzar.

Deep calls to deep in the roar of your cataracts,
all your waves and breakers swept over me.

By day the Lord will send his loving kindness,
at night his song shall be with me, a prayer to the God of my life.

I will say to God, my rock, 'Why have you forgotten me?

Why must I go about mournfully, oppressed by
   the enemy?'

My enemies taunt me, as if crushing my bones,
as all day long they ask me, 'Where is your God?'

Why are you cast down my soul, and why do you
   moan within me?
Hope in God! I praise Him still, my own
   salvation, and my God.

Psalm 42

The day of the funeral

O Lord,
who healest the broken hearted
and bindest up their wounds,
grant thy consolation unto mourners.
O strengthen and support them
in their day of grief and sorrow;
remember them (and their children)
for a long and good life. Put into their hearts the
   fear and love of thee;
that they may serve thee with a perfect heart
and let their latter end be peace.

From the Jewish Authorised Daily Prayer Book

Almighty God, who hast taught us that they who mourn shall be comforted; grant that in all our grief we may turn to thee; and, because our need is beyond the help of men, grant us the peace of thy consolation and the joy of thy love; through Jesus Christ our Lord.

Bishop Slattery

Heavenly Father,
on this sad and proud day we look to you in hope.
We dare to trust you alone.
Help us to believe that death is a gateway to what
 cannot be a lesser life;
assure us that he/she is safe in your keeping.
Spare us from the selfishness of living in the past,
and the luxury of private grief.
Rather, teach us to live out our lives gently with
 others,
and to trust that he/she will never be far from us
till the day when we all stand together before you.
Through Jesus Christ, our Lord.

Contemporary Prayers for Public Worship

IV

Anger and guilt

After the immediate shock of death, we can be hit by almost uncontrollable feelings of anger and guilt — anger against God, doctors, nurses and hospitals, or against ourselves. In regard to ourselves, this also includes feelings of guilt: I could have done more, I never gave enough love, 'if only...'

It is important both for now and future that we express ourselves fully. What we think or say about God may seem blasphemous, but to express it and have it out of our being is healing. God is patient and full of compassion. He will absorb your anger.

Guilt is less easy. How can we persuade ourselves that we are all right in relation to the one who has died? Again it is probably best to allow that guilt to surface, to let go. God still loves us in all this; nothing of the past can be changed; and the one we love now knows everything — and loves us more deeply than ever before.

Prayers

Lord, at this moment I feel I hate you. I am choked with anger and bitterness at you and anger and guilt towards myself. How could you not answer my prayer? How could you let him die? We were so close, the children are so young. What am I going to do? How can I be mother and father? How can I cope? And as to myself — I am angry that I wasted so much time, that I missed opportunities to work and love and show my love. Oh, I feel so guilty too. Perhaps I could have done more for him while he was ill — not been so irritable, so selfish, so hard. Lord, I can't sleep at night for anger, bitterness and guilt. Help me to get it out! Help me to be sane again. There is so much to do!

Why? Why? I cry and rage! Why had my son to die so young? Why not me if you had to take any of my family, and why one of us anyway? We are not perfect but are so much better than many in today's world. Show me why? Why will I not be able to see him in maturity and be able to play with the children he might have had? It is not fair. I ask you again why?

As David went, thus he said, 'O my son, Absolom,

my son; my son Absolom, would God I had died for thee O Absolom my son, my son.'

2 Sam 18:33

I am so very old, so blind that I cannot read, and my friends are all gone. Could you not have taken me instead of my son? I would gladly have died, for I am useless and I long to come to you. Lord, your ways are strange!

Though I grieve and weep and swear at you, your love wraps me round like a warm blanket on a cold night!

Lord, I am sure he let himself die because he did not want to be a burden which he thought he had been for several years. I did not think so at the time but perhaps in a way he was right, for looking back I can see that my life was rather limited then. I couldn't travel much with him, though we both enjoyed travelling. Sometimes now as I go on long trips to places he always wanted to see, I feel guilty. But then I realise that this is what he wanted me to do when he did not fight to live. I am grateful to him for his unselfish love and to you, Lord, for all your goodness to us. Amen.

Lord, the pain of loss is very great and life seems to have little meaning. I cannot believe I will not see her/him again. Everything here reminds me of her/him, and even if I go away for a break the memories return when I come back.

Then I keep recalling the unkind things I said and did; and, though they were not many, I wish I had not said or done them. Then I think if we had led quieter lives she/he might have lived longer!

I ask forgiveness for all my failures. I know there is nothing I can do to change the past, and the best way of accepting forgiveness is to take up the threads of life again and be thankful for the good times we had together.

Comfort and support me in my loneliness with the sense of your presence, and give me deeper understanding.

Day passes, night comes; morning comes, day passes, night comes...this is our life and our living, Lord. You are the maker of day and night. You rule the sun, the moon and the stars. At this time I do not find it easy or of any meaning to tell myself you are about when day passes and night comes and everything goes on rather like clockwork. It is so impersonal, Lord. I feel I want to shout out: 'Can you hear me, Lord?'...and sometimes I do. And still you are silent, and morning comes, day passes — where are you, Lord?

And the Lord answers: 'I am in your heart.'

V

Is there a life after death?

At the time of death we may wonder where the persons have gone. Are they near us or are they with God? If they are with God, are they far removed from us? Sometimes the dead seem very close and at other times completely gone from us. It is good at such times to question God. And it helps to look at the ways others have seen death as the gateway to a fuller life which unites us, them and God more closely.

Prayers and thoughts

Where are you God?
Sometimes I wonder Lord,
If when we die we go
To be with you; but where
Are you? We know
From experience that you are

With us, but do you cease to be
When we die? Lord help me
to understand a little better.
Are you 'out there'
Or only 'in me'?
Help me; it's so hard
for us to understand.

Think...
Of stepping on shore, and finding it heaven.
Of taking hold of a hand, and finding it God's hand.
Of breathing a new air, and finding it celestial air.
Of feeling invigorated, and finding it immortality.
Of passing from storm and tempest to an
   unbroken calm.
Of waking up and, and finding it Home.

Anonymous

When I am overwhelmed by the death of a friend, help me, Lord, to remember Jacob's dream of the ladder ascending to heaven with angels coming down and going up from earth to heaven. You made heaven and earth very close, and you have through the life, death, and resurrection of your Son made them even closer.

The whole earth provides a taking off place to you if we can but see this and let ourselves experience it; even the humblest part of creation is touched by your glory if we keep our eyes open. You are with me now in my sorrow and bewilderment, though I do not understand how; help me to realise that you never leave me.

As the moorland pool images the sun, so in our hours of self-giving thou shinest on us, and we mirror thee to men. But of the other land, our heaven to be, we have no picture at all. Only we know that thou art there. And Jesus the door and the welcome of each faithful one.

Alistair Maclean

VI

Realising loss and learning to live in hope

When we have lost someone we love, there is no way we can reverse the situation. Death is final. Normally, however, it takes time for our loss to sink into the centre of our being — for us to realise fully the pain, the gap and the loneliness. Then it really hits us!

We must gradually learn to live in and with this new situation. We must live it in slowly dawning hope for the peace and joy of the one we love who has gone to God; and for the possibilities in our own life without their presence, yet peaceful and positive in relation to God and our friends, relations and neighbours.

Prayers and thoughts

We seem to give them back to thee, O God, who gavest them to us. Yet as thou didst not lose them in giving, so we do not lose them by their return. Not as the world giveth, givest thou, O lover of souls. What thou givest, thou takest not away, for what is thine is ours also if we are thine. And life is eternal and love is immortal, and death is only an horizon, and an horizon is nothing save the limit of our sight. Lift us up, strong Son of God, that we may see further; cleanse our eyes that we may see more clearly; draw us closer to thyself that we may know ourselves to be nearer to our loved ones who are with thee. And while thou dost prepare a place for us, prepare us also for that happy place, that where thou art we may be also for evermore. Amen.

Anonymous

He said not: thou shalt not be tempested, thou shalt not be travailed, thou shalt not be afflicted; but he said: thou shalt not be overcome.

Mother Julian of Norwich

Let us thank God for the years they were with us; for the gaiety and happiness and the companionship and love they gave us.

These are things that nothing can take away, they are ours to hold in our hearts and cherish all the days of our life.

Let us dwell on these things and not on the sadness of a temporary farewell.

Selwyn Cumnor

Lord, now the family have gone I have a great sense of emptiness and an even greater sense of loss. They shared my grief and we supported each other. I miss this sharing dreadfully and am now so very alone. The future looms like a great useless void, and full, if a void can be full, of pain and senseless living. Lord, do not let me be overcome by this; give me some hope!

So many of those I love have died and gone from the present touch and reality of the today in which we live, Lord. I get so sad. There are some, I know, who cannot believe they will ever meet again the love of their life; there are those who are full of dismay, emptiness and loss. In my own grief I pray for these, Lord Jesus. Let your Spirit bring them understanding and peace. For those who do believe in life after death, please strengthen their belief so that they can strengthen others. For me, Lord, at this time of loss, I just ask you to hold me in the darkness so that I may not lose a sense of the hereafter in my tears. Jesus, you said

to Martha: 'I am the resurrection and the life'...
Help me to believe this!

Lord, people avoid me as if I had some unclean disease. Are they afraid that I will talk of my sorrow and weep in the street? How could I do this with someone I know only superficially? But Lord, I long for a friend who would listen when I talked about him and who would remember with me the things he said and did. It helps to recall what he was like and the good things that happened. To do this is not morbid, though some think it is. Lord, encourage my friends to visit me and to listen and share. Amen.

You called Abraham from his home.
You led the Israelites into the wilderness
where they wandered for many years
before they entered the promised land.
I am in a desert now, not
knowing where you are taking me.
Often I do not know that I am
being led anywhere — I seem to go in circles!
I forget the Spirit who guides me
blows where he wills like the elusive wind
that seems to have no purpose.
I like to see where I am going;

I prefer security, but you have never
given your people this.
You have taken everything from me
and I live a hand to mouth existence.
Is this what you want of me?
Will I like Moses see something
of your glory in my particular desert?
Spirit of love and truth, guide me
to your abiding city.

Though I am dead grieve not for me with tears.
Think not of death with sorrowing and tears;
I am so near that every tear you shed touches and
tortures me though you think me dead.
But when you laugh and sing in glad delight,
   my soul is
lifted upwards to the light.
Laugh and be glad for all life is giving and I,
though dead will share your joy in living.

Anonymous

Give me that peace which you gave to the disciples after you had been raised from the dead. You gave them a deep peace which sprang from their belief and trust in you and in the power of your Spirit. They were able to go out to tell the world about you and your love for all because they were rooted and grounded in you. Give me that peace which is unshakeable however disturbed and unhappy I and the world may be.

I cannot believe he is gone. I still expect him to come in, or find him sitting on the sofa ready to hear my news when I come in from shopping. When he is not there I experience a great let-down, though I still retain a sense of waiting for his return. It is cruel! Help me, Lord, to accept that from henceforth I will be on my own.

It is very lonely on my own, Lord; but generally with your support I have come to live peacefully and contentedly. There are times when I feel my loss particularly: when I arrive at an airport or station and other people are being met, I have to go on alone. It is then I seem so much on my own and my heart aches. At such times I do miss human companionship, though you support me wonderfully and I have good friends for whom I am deeply grateful.

We pray for them not because God will otherwise neglect them. We pray for them because we know He loves and cares for them, and we claim the privilege of uniting our love with God's.

But do not be content to pray for them. Let us also ask them to pray for us. In such prayers while they lived on earth they both displayed and consecrated their love towards us. Doubtless that ministry of love continues; but let us seek it, ask for it, claim it. It is in the mutual service of prayer, our prayer for them and theirs for us, that we come closest to them.

William Temple

Lord, come alive within me,
within my sorrow and disappointment and doubts,
within the ordinary movements of my life.
Come alive as the peace and joy and assurance
   that is
stronger than the locked doors within with which
I try to shut out life.
Come alive as the peace and joy and assurance that
nothing can kill.

Rex Chapman

As the rain hides the stars, as the autumn mist hides the hills, as the clouds veil the blue of the sky, so the dark happenings of my lot hide the shining of thy face from me. Yet, if I may hold thy hand in the darkness, it is enough. Since I know that, though I may stumble in my going, thou dost not fall.

Alistair Maclean

I know that all who love Jesus Christ are united by his Spirit and I thank you, Lord, for this knowledge. I know that in prayer I hold those who have died, in you, in your love, and they hold me in this way too. I do not know whether humanly this is called praying with or for the dead, but I know it is the way I pray with and for those who are my friends in this life. Lord, continue to give me the great grace of experiencing this union in you with all those I love, whether alive or dead, and help me to explain to others the wonder and warmth of this way of prayer. Amen.

VII

Resurrection

Jesus died and rose from the grave. As St Paul says, if he did not rise, then our faith is vain. This faith I hope we share about those who have died and about ourselves after death.

The immediate resurrection after bereavement is different. In this sense, resurrection refers to our personal rising from the death of bereavement. After a period of bewilderment, life must go on again in a new way. This, I am sure, is what our dead friend or relation would want for us — our growth, happiness and joy.

So let us go forward into this new life of resurrection until we come to our own death and resurrection to eternal life.

Prayers and thoughts

If I should die and leave you here awhile,
Be not like others, sore undone, who keep

Long vigils by the silent dust, and weep.
For my sake, turn again to life and smile,
Nerving thy heart and trembling hand to do
Something to comfort weaker hearts than thine.
Complete those dear unfinished tasks of mine,
And I perchance may therein comfort you.

A. Price Hughes

Lord, my loved ones are near me.
I know that they live in the shadow.
My eyes can't see them because they have left for a moment
their bodies as one leaves behind outmoded clothing.
Their souls, deprived of their disguise, no longer communicate with me.

But in you, Lord, I hear them calling me.
I see them beckoning to me.
I hear them giving me advice.
For they are now more vividly present.
Before, our bodies touched but not our souls.
Now I meet them when I meet you.
I receive them when I receive you.
I love them when I love you.
O, my loved ones, eternally alive, who live in me,
Help me to learn thoroughly in this short life how to live eternally.

Lord, I love you, and I want to love you more.
It's you who makes love eternal, and I want to
   love eternally.

Michel Quoist

Lord, I see resurrection is bound up with love: you were raised because you died in love; I am raised when, in love, I die to myself. Resurrection gives a new colour to living; the glow of dawn touches my heart and gives me hope and transforms all things and all my relationships with others. It brings hope that I will know you in the sunshine of paradise. The last dying will bring me to you, the everlasting love and light.

There we shall rest and we shall see.
We shall see and we shall love.
We shall love and we shall praise.
Behold what shall be in the end
and shall not end.

St Augustine

The fall doth pass the rise in worth:
for birth hath in itself the germ of death,
but death has in itself the germ of birth.
It is the falling acorn buds the tree,
the falling rain that bears the greenery;
the fern plants moulder when the ferns arise,

for there is nothing lives but something dies.
And there is nothing dies but something lives,
till skies be fugitives.

Francis Thompson

In God we live and move and have our being. Alive or dead, we are all in him. It would be more true to say that we are all alive in him, and that there is no death. Our God is not the God of the dead but of the living. He is your God, he is the God of her/him who has died. There is only one God, and in this one God you are both united. Only you cannot see each other for the time being. But this means your future meeting will be the more joyful; and then no one will take your joy from you. Yet even now you live together; all that has happened is that she/he has gone into another room and closed the door... Spiritual love transcends visible separation.

S. Tyszkiewicz and T. Belpaire

Death of Charles Williams

My friendship is not ended, his death has had the very unexpected effect of making death look quite different.

I believe in the next life ten times more strongly

than I did... It is not blasphemous to believe that what was true of our Lord is, in a less degree, true of all who are in him.

They go away in order to be *with* us in a new way even closer than before.

Williams says about the death of his wife, 'She was dead but her very death heightened that word supernatural'.

C.S. Lewis

Death is nothing at all, I have only slipped away into the next room.

I am I and you are you, whatever we were to each other we are still.

Call me by my old familiar name, speak to me in the easy way which we always used.

Put no difference in your tone; wear no forced air of solemnity or sorrow.

Laugh as we always laughed at little jokes together.

Pray, smile, think of me, pray for me.

Let my name be ever the household word that it always was, let it be spoken without the effort, without the trace of a shadow in it.

Life means all that it ever meant, it is the same as it ever was; there is absolutely unbroken continuity.

What is death but a negligible accident? Why should I be out of mind because I am out of sight? I am but waiting for you, for an interval somewhere very near, just round the corner.

All is well.

Henry Scott Holland

Short prayers

We include these short prayers because it can be a great help to us during sickness, watching over a sick person and in bereavement to have these small ejaculatory prayers which we can come to love, and find easily rising from our hearts to our lips.

There are many more. You can make up your own — and hopefully you can share them among yourselves, the sick and the well having a common prayer which each knows the other is saying when apart and which they can use and share when together.

Support and strengthen me, Lord!

Lord, he whom you love is ill. *(Jn 11:3)*

Lord, help me to keep going!

With you, all things are possible.

Be it unto me according to your will.

Lord, though you slay me yet will I trust.
(Job 13:15 [AV])

I am hopeless and helpless — help me!

Love is not changed by death
— and nothing is lost,
and all in the end is harvest. *(Edith Sitwell)*

Death is not extinguishing the Light,
but putting out the Lamp because the dawn
   has come. *(R. Tagore)*

The dead are no further than God
and God is very near. *(Author unknown)*

Lord who has given all for us, help us to give
   all for you. *(G.W. Biggs)*

You bore the pain of the cross; please help me
   bear this agony.

The memory of the righteous is a blessing.
(Jewish prayer)

Epilogue

We will Remember Them

They shall not grow old, as we who are left
  grow old:
Age shall not weary them, nor the years condemn.
At the going down of the sun and in the morning
We will remember them.

Laurence Binyon

O God, help me to remember in my grief that neither death nor life, nor angels, nor principalities, nor powers, nor things present, nor things to come, nor heights, nor depths, nor any other creature is able to separate me from your love which is in Christ Jesus our Lord.

Acknowledgements

The publishers would like to express their gratitude to the following for use of their copyright material:

Allen and Unwin Ltd, for the quote from C.S. Lewis from *Inklings* by Humphrey Carpenter ©1978. Used with permission.

W. & R. Chambers Ltd, for the extracts from *Hebridean Altars* by Alistair Maclean ©1937. Used with permission.

The Episcopal Church of Scotland (Publications Committee), for Psalm 23 from the *Scottish Psalter 1650*. Used with permission.

Extract from the Authorized King James Version of the Bible is Crown Copyright in the United Kingdom and is reproduced by permission of Eyre & Spottiswoode (Publishers) Limited Her Majesty's Printers.

Gill and Macmillan Ltd, for the extract from 'The Funeral' from Michel Quoist's *Prayers of Life* ©1965. Reproduced with permission.

Macmillans Ltd, for the extract from the writings of Rabindrath Tagore and for the extract from the writings of Archbishop William Temple. Used with permission.

Oxford University Press, for the extract from the *London Service Book* edited by W. Briggs ©1948. Used with permission.

Colin Murray Parkes for the extract from *All In the End Is Harvest* ©1984.

Soncino Press Ltd, for the extract from the *Authorised Daily Prayer Book* edited by J.H. Hertz.

SCM Press Ltd, for the extract from *Contemporary Prayers for Public Worship* edited by Caryl Micklem ©1967, and the extract from *A Kind of Praying* by Rex Chapman ©1970. Used with permission.

Mrs Nicolete Gray and the Society of Authors on behalf of the Laurence Binyon Estate for the extract from *For the Fallen* (September 1914) by Laurence Binyon. Used with permission.

NOTES

NOTES